Jamie's Red Nose

CW00410027

Any-way-you-like cookies   6

Tea-party fairy cakes   8

My nan's lemon drizzle cake   10

Banana & blueberry French toast   12

Homemade granola with berry compote   15

Salad from Capri   16

Sausage carbonara   18

My old man's superb chicken   21

Cottage pie with vegetables   22

Tasty fish bake   25

Chicken korma   26

Easy peasy ginger beer   28

Hi guys

Big thanks for buying my little Red Nose Day recipe book. This is the third time I've done something like this with Comic Relief, and hopefully this year we'll raise more money than ever!

This Red Nose Day is a chance for us to completely change millions of people's lives for the better – not bad for a day of mucking around, making some great food and having a laugh! The good people at Comic Relief always find wonderful deserving causes to support and this year the cash will go towards a load of different projects. Just to give you one example, some of the money raised will go towards fighting malaria. Living in the UK means most of us hear about this disease only if we go on holiday and need a vaccination. But in Africa malaria kills a child every 30 seconds, which adds up to a staggering one million lives lost every year. But actually, because the disease is transmitted by mosquitoes, there are several simple and cheap ways of fighting it. For instance, a bed net to protect a mother and child only costs five quid.

I know for a fact that Friday 13 March 2009 will make a massive difference because I've seen for myself what Comic Relief money can do. When I visited South Africa a few years ago I was blown away by the beautiful people I met and the incredible things your money has achieved there. That helped me realize how

absolutely necessary it is for us to keep giving as much as possible.

You've already done something great by buying this book, so nice one! But this year I reckon we should all go that little bit further. Why not rope in a few of your mates and use the recipes here as a starting point for raising some serious cash? The lovely little fairy cakes and cookies in this book are the type of thing you'll be able to knock together in no time and then sell to people at your school or work to raise money for those less fortunate than yourselves.

As well as those, you'll also find some of my favourite meals in here. There's my old man's superb chicken – still so delicious, even after all these years – some hearty family pies, a really

cracking curry and some great little brekkie ideas that the kids will love. You can host a bash for cash on Red Nose Day and cook with your friends and family. It's a fantastic way to raise money, especially if you can persuade your guests to learn a new recipe and promise to Pass It On (see page 5). What a brilliant combination!

In many ways, Red Nose Day and cooking are similar: both are fun, both are better with mates around and both should inspire you to get creative.

So however you decide to raise your cash, have a fantastic Red Nose Day!

Love

Jamie

Pass It On

Anyone can learn how to cook something – all they have to do is give it a try. That's what Pass It On is all about. It's part of my Ministry of Food movement to get the nation cooking again. Cooking real food from scratch is much better for you than surviving on takeaways! Plus, it can be loads of fun, especially if your mates can't cook.

The idea behind Pass It On is simple: learn a few recipes (I've stuck a Red Nose on the really easy ones to get you started!), practise them in your own home first, then pass them on by teaching them to at least two of your friends or family who can't cook. Then, most importantly, get them to promise that they'll teach their mates and so on, and so on, until everyone can cook . . . It's easy, it's fun, and it could change the way Britain eats!

So, on Red Nose Day, host a bash for cash, make some of these delicious recipes and pass them on at the same time.

There are more loads more recipes, videos and advice about how to organize a Pass It On event on my website:

www.jamiesministryoffood.com

Any-way-you-like cookies easy

makes about 20 cookies

This is a basic cookie dough recipe, with a few added oats for a bit of a twist. I'm giving you two options – pick the flavour you fancy the most and it'll be enough for a whole batch of cookies. Perfect for a Red Nose Day bake sale!

for the basic cookie dough
115g butter, softened
100g unrefined golden caster sugar
1 large free-range or organic egg
100g plain flour, sifted
20g porridge oats
½ teaspoon baking powder
½ teaspoon salt

for white chocolate and ginger cookies
80g white chocolate, chopped
30g stem ginger in syrup, drained
 and finely chopped

for dark chocolate and orange cookies
80g dark chocolate, chopped
zest of 2 unwaxed oranges

Place all the basic cookie dough ingredients in a food processor and mix until smooth and creamy. If you don't have a food processor, just cream together the butter and sugar by hand, then add the egg, beating all the time before adding the remaining ingredients.

Stir your chosen flavours into the cookie mix, then spoon the mix on to a piece of clingfilm and roll into a sausage shape with a 7cm diameter. Chill in the freezer for 20 minutes.

Preheat the oven to 180°C/350°F/gas 4. Cut 1cm slices off the chilled cookie dough. Place onto 2 non-stick baking trays, leaving a good space in between each one – they'll spread while they're cooking. If you can't fit them all on the trays, just cook another batch. Bake for 8 to 10 minutes until the edges are golden brown. Cool slightly before placing on a wire rack to cool and crisp up. Delicious with a glass of cold milk.

Tip: If you fancy dried fruit and nuts instead of chocolate and ginger or chocolate and orange, feel free to use them, but keep the quantities the same.

A SOU
OF THE COR
H.M. QUEEN

Tea-party fairy cakes *makes 18 cakes*

easy

These are great fairy cakes to bake for your Red Nose Day bake sale, or to serve at tea-parties. You can use a variety of icings and toppings – I'm giving you my favourites. You'll need two 12-bun muffin tins and some paper cases.

for the sponge
225g unsalted butter, softened
225g self-raising flour, sifted
225g caster sugar
4 large free-range or organic eggs
zest of 1 lemon
optional extra toppings: crystallized
  flower petals, dried cranberries,
  slivered almonds, pistachio nuts

for the fresh fruit icing
50g fresh berries (raspberries,
  strawberries, blueberries or
  blackberries), plus extra fruit for
  decoration
150g icing sugar, sifted

for the chocolate icing
150g icing sugar, sifted
4 tablespoons cocoa powder, sifted

for the orange icing
150g icing sugar, sifted
zest of 1 orange
1–2 tablespoons orange juice

To make your sponge mixture, preheat the oven to 180°C/350°F/gas 4. Beat the butter and sugar together, either using an electric whisk or by hand with a wooden spoon, until very light and fluffy. Add the eggs one at a time, beating each one before you add the next, then fold in the flour and lemon zest. Then place 18 paper cases into your muffin tins, and evenly spoon the mixture into them. Put the muffin tins into the oven and bake for 15 minutes. Check to see if the cakes are cooked by poking a cocktail stick right into one of them. Remove it after 5 seconds and if comes out clean they're cooked; if slightly sticky they'll need a bit longer, so put them back in the oven for another 5 minutes, or until cooked through and golden on top. If cooked too long, though, they'll just go dry, so keep an eye on them. Remove the cakes from the tins and let them cool on a rack.

Now make your icing. The ingredients given for each icing make enough to cover all the fairy cakes. Decide whether you want to stick to one flavour for all your cakes, or reduce the quantities so you can have a few of each flavour.

To make the fresh fruit icing, mash up your chosen berries with a fork or whiz them in a food processor. If the fruit has pips you may want to pass it through a sieve. Mix in the sifted icing sugar until you have a smooth paste.

To make the chocolate icing, mix together the icing sugar, cocoa powder and 60ml water until you have a smooth paste.

To make the orange icing, mix the icing sugar with the orange zest. Gradually add your orange juice until you have a nice smooth paste.

When the cakes have cooled, drizzle a teaspoon of your chosen icing over each one and top with berries, crystallized flower petals, dried cranberries, slivered almonds or pistachio nuts. Even better, stick a strawberry on the top to give each one a red nose.

My nan's lemon drizzle cake serves 8–10

This great old-fashioned tea cake is also perfectly presentable as a dessert with a big serving of ice cream.

for the sponge
115g unsalted butter, softened
115g caster sugar
4 large free-range or organic eggs
180g ground almonds
30g poppy seeds
zest and juice of 2 lemons
125g self-raising flour, sifted

for the lemon syrup
100g caster sugar
90g lemon juice

for the lemon icing
225g icing sugar
zest and juice of 1 lemon

Preheat the oven to 180°C/350°F/gas 4. Grease and line the bottom and sides of a 20cm springform cake tin with greaseproof paper.

Using an electric whisk, beat the butter with the caster sugar until light and creamy. Add the eggs one by one, beating each in well. Fold in the ground almonds, poppy seeds, lemon zest and juice and the sifted flour. Spoon the mix into the prepared cake tin and bake in the preheated oven for 40 minutes or until lightly golden. You can check if the cake is cooked by poking a cocktail stick right into the sponge. Remove it after 5 seconds, and if it comes out clean the cake is cooked; if slightly sticky it needs a little longer, so put it back in the oven. Allow the cake to cool on a rack.

Make your lemon syrup by heating the sugar and lemon juice in a pan until the sugar has dissolved. While your cake is still warm, make lots of little holes in the top with a cocktail stick and pour your syrup over.

To make your icing, sift the icing sugar into a bowl and add the lemon zest and juice, stirring until smooth. When your cake is almost cool, put it on a serving plate and pour the icing carefully over the top, letting gravity disperse it down the sides, giving you the 'drizzle' effect! Give it a helping hand with a spoon if you want.

Banana & blueberry French toast *serves 1* *easy*

This is the kind of sandwich that can be eaten for breakfast or even for dessert. Feel free to vary the fruit that you use – my missus likes strawberries and bananas, while my daughter Poppy prefers banana with blackberries and blueberries.

2 slices of nice medium-cut
  white bread
butter
a handful of mixed berries, fresh
  or frozen
runny honey or caster sugar
optional: ½ a banana, roughly
  mashed

2 large free-range or organic eggs
a splash of milk
icing sugar, for dusting
crème fraîche, cream or ice cream,
  to serve

Butter your slices of bread thinly on both sides. Toss your berries in a little honey or sugar just to sweeten them a bit. A little mashed banana holds it all together quite nicely.

Beat a couple of eggs in a bowl with a couple of tablespoons of caster sugar and a splash of milk, then dip both slices of bread in the sweet egg mixture so it's egged on both sides. Let the excess drip off, then smear the fruit mixture on one slice, leaving a slight space around the edges of the bread. Put the other slice on top and press down. The egg will help the fruit to stick.

Fry in a little butter in a medium hot pan on both sides, pushing down gently so that the fruit is pressed into the bread. Once the bread is golden and slightly crisp, dust with icing sugar and serve with a dollop of crème fraîche, cream or ice cream and any remaining fruit mixture spooned over.

Homemade granola with berry compote

easy

serves 6

The brilliant thing about granola, aside from the fact that it's full of good-for-you things, is that it's wonderfully versatile. Depending on your mood, you can have it for a treat, or breakfast. Any leftover granola will keep happily in an airtight container for about a month, but it never lasts longer than a week at mine.

200g mixed nuts
400g rolled or jumbo oats
100g pumpkin and/or sunflower seeds
400g runny honey
200g strawberries, hulled and halved
200g raspberries
200g mixed dried fruit (raisins, blueberries, cranberries, cherries, chopped apricots)
500ml plain yoghurt

Preheat your oven to 180°C/350°F/gas 4. Put the nuts into a plastic bag, squeeze the air out and seal the bag. Gently bash the bag with a rolling pin until the nuts are lightly crushed, then tip them into a mixing bowl and add the oats and seeds. Warm up the honey to make it extra runny and stir it into the oaty mixture with a wooden spoon until everything's lightly coated.

Tip the mixture on to a baking tray and spread out roughly with the wooden spoon. Place the tray in the preheated oven and bake for about 30 minutes, until the mixture is crunchy and a dark golden brown. Meanwhile, place the strawberries and raspberries in a pan on a medium heat for 10 minutes until nicely stewed.

Remove the tray from the oven and allow to cool, then break up the toasted seeds, oats and nuts into clumps and mix in the dried fruit. There you have it: granola!

Serve the granola in small bowls or glasses. Top with the plain yoghurt and the hot fruit compote.

Salad from Capri *serves 4* easy

This is my take on a traditional Italian recipe. It tastes absolutely delicious and has to be one of the simplest salads you can make.

4 x 150g balls of buffalo mozzarella
2 handfuls of good mixed tomatoes, of different shapes and sizes
the white of 1 spring onion, very finely sliced
extra virgin olive oil
good-quality herb vinegar
freshly ground black pepper

for the dressing
a big handful of fresh basil leaves
sea salt
extra virgin olive oil

First, make your dressing. Keeping a few leaves aside for later, roughly chop the basil and pound with a good pinch of salt in a pestle and mortar. Add a splash of oil and stir it in to make a lovely smashed basil dressing.

Carefully tear the mozzarella on to a large serving plate. Chop the tomatoes roughly into chunks and dress in a bowl with the spring onion, some olive oil, a little herb vinegar and some salt and pepper. Place the tomatoes in and around the mozzarella and drizzle the basil sauce over the top. Sprinkle with the reserved basil leaves and serve.

Sausage Carbonara *serves 4* *easy*

This is like having a breakfast dish of pasta and it's absolutely delicious! Not only does it look impressive but it's so quick to make.

4 good-quality organic Italian sausages
olive oil
4 slices of thickly cut pancetta, chopped
sea salt and freshly ground black pepper
455g dried linguine
4 large egg yolks, preferably free-range or organic
100ml double cream
100ml freshly grated Parmesan cheese
zest of 1 lemon
a sprig of fresh flat-leaf parsley, chopped
extra virgin olive oil

With a sharp knife, slit the sausage skins lengthways and pop all the meat out. Using wet hands, roll little balls of sausage meat about the size of large marbles and place them to one side.

Heat a large frying pan and add a good splash of olive oil. Gently fry the sausage meatballs until golden brown all over, then add the pancetta and continue to cook for a couple of minutes, until it's golden. While this is cooking, bring a pan of salted water to the boil, add the linguine and cook according to the packet instructions.

In a large bowl, whip up the egg yolks, cream, half the Parmesan, the lemon zest and parsley. When the pasta is cooked, drain it in a colander, reserving a little of the cooking water, and immediately toss it quickly with the egg mixture back in the pasta pan. Add the hot sausage meatballs and toss everything together. The egg will cook delicately from the heat of the linguine, just enough for it to thicken and not scramble. The sauce should be smooth and silky. If the pasta becomes a little claggy, add a few spoonfuls of the reserved cooking water to loosen it slightly. Sprinkle over the rest of the Parmesan, season if necessary, drizzle with extra virgin olive oil and serve. Eat immediately!

My old man's superb chicken *serves 4*

I've been making this chicken recipe of my dad's for years now and it's never let me down. It's beautiful to look at and even better to eat.

170g mushrooms, any combination
olive oil
1 or 2 cloves of garlic, peeled and finely chopped
sea salt and freshly ground black pepper
1 handful of fresh flat-leaf parsley, chopped
4 x 200g skinless chicken breasts, preferably free-range or organic
plain flour, for dusting
1 x 500g pack of puff pastry
1 large free-range or organic egg, beaten
2 heaped tablespoons wholegrain mustard
1 large wineglass of white wine
140ml double cream

Preheat the oven to 200°C/400°F/gas 6. Chop up the mushrooms – half rough and half fine. To a hot pan, add a couple of lugs of olive oil and slowly fry the garlic with the mushrooms for about 10 minutes. Season to taste and stir in the chopped parsley. Allow to cool. Pull back the chicken fillet on the breast and, keeping it intact, score into the breast and stuff the chicken with the cooled mushrooms.

Using a little dusting of flour and a rolling-pin, roll the pastry out to around 45cm in length, 20cm wide and just over 0.5cm thick. Slice into 4 pieces lengthways and wrap around each chicken breast. Brush the pastry with a little egg and cook in the preheated oven for 35 minutes.

While the chicken is cooking, put the mustard and white wine into a hot pan and allow to reduce until you've cooked away the alcohol smell. Add the cream and simmer until the sauce coats the back of a spoon, then remove from the heat and season to taste. When the chicken breasts have cooked, remove from the oven, slice each breast into 3 and serve with a bit of sauce and a drizzle of olive oil if you like. Gorgeous!

Cottage pie with vegetables *serves 4*

easy

A real favourite any time of the year – and the extra veg will help with your five portions a day. If you like, try mixing a little grated Cheddar cheese into your mash for a tasty topping.

olive oil
1 small red onion, peeled and finely chopped
2 carrots, peeled and diced
¼ of a small swede, peeled and diced
2 parsnips, peeled and diced
2 sprigs of fresh rosemary
2 bay leaves
500g minced beef
sea salt and freshly ground black pepper
250ml beef stock
100g frozen peas
1kg potatoes, peeled and chopped into even-sized pieces
75g butter

Preheat the oven to 180°C/350°F/gas 4. Heat a large saucepan over a medium heat and pour in a splash of olive oil. Add the onion, carrots, swede, parsnips, one of the rosemary sprigs and the bay leaves. Cook gently with the lid on until soft.

Turn the heat up, crumble in the mince and fry until lightly browned. Season well with salt and pepper, add the stock and bring to the boil. Turn the heat back down to medium and simmer for half an hour before stirring in the peas.

Boil the potatoes in salted water until soft, then drain and mash with the butter and plenty of salt and pepper. Remove the rosemary and bay leaves from the pan, then tip the mince into a baking dish and cover with the mash.

Break the remaining rosemary sprig into pieces and toss them in a little olive oil to coat them and stop them burning. Poke them into the mash, sprinkle with salt and bake in the preheated oven for 25 minutes until piping hot and crispy on top.

Tasty fish bake *serves 4*

This dish makes wonderful use of trout (as I've used here), sardines, salmon or mackerel – any fish really, but oily ones are great to use, especially for kids. Try to get hold of the freshest fish you can, and ask your fishmonger to prepare it and get rid of the bones for you.

400g potatoes, scrubbed and finely sliced
4 tablespoons olive oil
1 clove of garlic, peeled and chopped
1 onion, peeled and sliced
1 bulb of fennel, trimmed and sliced
1 teaspoon fennel seeds
4 medium or 8 small fillets of trout, scaled and pinboned
285ml single cream
2 handfuls of freshly grated Parmesan cheese, plus extra for sprinkling
2 anchovy fillets, chopped
sea salt and freshly ground black pepper
2 handfuls of fresh breadcrumbs
2 lemons, halved

Preheat the oven to 200°C/400°F/gas 6. First of all, parboil the sliced potatoes in salted boiling water for a few minutes until softened and then drain in a colander. Place a 20cm casserole-type pan on a low heat and add the oil, garlic, onion, fennel and fennel seeds. Cook slowly for 10 minutes with the lid on, stirring every so often.

Take the pan off the heat. Lay your trout fillets skin-side up over the onion and fennel. Mix together your cream, Parmesan and anchovies, season with salt and freshly ground black pepper, and pour over the fish. Toss the potato slices in a little olive oil, salt and pepper and layer these over the top. Place in the oven for 20 minutes, sprinkling with the breadcrumbs and a little grated Parmesan 5 minutes before the end. Serve with lemon halves, a green salad and some cold beers for the adults!

Chicken Korma *serves 4–6*

easy

This much-loved curry has a slightly mild, creamy taste, which makes it a great one for kids to try. Because I love fresh chillies I've added one here, but traditional kormas don't include them, so feel free to leave it out. Kormas are also absolutely delicious made with prawns.

4 skinless chicken breasts, preferably free-range or organic
2 medium onions
optional: 1 fresh green chilli
a thumb-sized piece of fresh root ginger
a small bunch of fresh coriander
groundnut or vegetable oil
a knob of butter
½ a 290g jar of Patak's korma curry paste
1 x 400ml tin of coconut milk

a small handful of flaked almonds, plus extra for serving
1 x 400g tin of chickpeas
2 heaped tablespoons desiccated coconut
sea salt and freshly ground black pepper
500g natural yoghurt
optional: 400g cooked basmati rice and some warmed poppadums
1 lemon

Cut the chicken into 3cm cubes. Peel, halve and finely slice your onions, then halve, deseed and finely slice the chilli if you're using it. Peel and finely chop the ginger, and pick the coriander leaves and finely chop the stalks.

Put a large casserole-type pan on a medium to high heat and add a couple of lugs of oil. Add the onions, chilli, ginger and coriander stalks with the butter. Cook for around 10 minutes and keep stirring it so it doesn't catch and burn, but turns evenly golden. Add the korma curry paste, coconut milk and flaked almonds and stir well to coat everything. Drain the chickpeas in a colander and add them to the pan with the desiccated coconut and sliced chicken breasts. Half fill the empty tin with water, pour it into the pan, and stir again. Bring to the boil, turn the heat down and simmer for 30 minutes with the lid on.

Check the curry regularly to make sure it's not drying out, and add extra water if necessary. When the chicken is tender and cooked, taste and season with salt and pepper if you think it needs it. Feel free to serve your curry with some cooked basmati rice, a few poppadums and a spoonful or two of natural yoghurt dolloped on top. Sprinkle over the rest of the flaked almonds and a few coriander leaves, and serve with lemon wedges for squeezing over.

Easy peasy ginger beer *serves 4–6*

easy

Ginger beer is one of my favourite things in the world, especially in the summer. I can't think of anything more sexy than having a big jug of iced ginger beer on the table with a barbecue on a hot day. Here's my short-cut for getting amazing results.

140g fresh ginger
4 tablespoons muscovado sugar
2–3 lemons
1 litre soda water or sparkling mineral
water
sprigs of fresh mint

First of all, you need to grate your ginger on a coarse cheese grater – you can leave the skin on if you like. Put the ginger with its pulpy juice into a bowl and sprinkle in your muscovado sugar. Remove the rind from 2 of your lemons with a vegetable peeler, add to the bowl, and slightly bash and squash with something heavy like a pestle or rolling-pin. Just do this for 10 seconds, to mix up all the flavours. Squeeze the juice from all 3 lemons and add most of it to the bowl. Pour in your fizzy water or soda water. Allow to sit for 10 minutes and then taste. You may feel that the lemons are too sour, therefore add a little more sugar; if it's slightly too sweet, add a little more lemon juice. To be honest, these amounts are always a bit variable, so just follow your taste. Pass the ginger beer through a coarse sieve into a large jug and adds lots of ice and some sprigs of mint.